The Author of
"Inner Struggles,
Peace & Blessings"

Kaprina Parham

POET / AUTHOR

443.675.6535

icyunvkp@gmail.com

WWW.KPPOETRY.COM

Inner Struggles

Peace &

Blessings

Kaprina Parham

ISBN: 978-1-095-77092-4

Contents

Introduction

Hi, my name is Kaprina Parham, "Kp". I am the mother of three children, Z'Adah, Za'Nia & Z'Aira. I was born and raised all over the city and suburbs of Baltimore, MD. As a child, I would read poetry written by Langston Hughes, Maya Angelou and others. Writing is my passion since the age of 13. My 1st poem was written the evening before Valentine's Day for a high school basketball player I had a crush on called, "A High School Crush". After writing that very 1st poem, my classmates requested revisions to be written for themselves to offer their crush and I was compensated. That was enough motivation to continue writing. I was the only 9th grade student in a 12th grade math class. A great beginning to not only writing, but as an Entrepreneur.

I encourage you to find your passion and develop it. You don't have to focus on only one thing. Your journey can take your craft(s) to another level.

Acknowledgements

I would like to thank you for your interest in this book entitled, "Inner Struggles, Peace & Blessings" and I hope you enjoy its content. I would like to thank God for installing visions, dreams, courage etc. to allow this to happen. I would like to thank my mother, children, brother Jimmy, grandmother, uncles, friends, JamesChase Media, David Chance and Dante Jordan of the R&B Group Ruff Endz, Comedian Alabama, Howard G, Michael Phelps, Author A. Sneed & a host of others for being not only an inspiration, but a support system for me.

A portion of proceeds will be contributed to NAMI of Baltimore.

Thank you,

Kaprina Parham

CHAPTER 1

I LOVE THE LORD

THANK YOU LORD FOR BLESSING ME THE WAY THAT YOU DO.

EVERYTHING I'VE WANTED IN LIFE IS BEGINNING TO SLOWLY COME TRUE.

YOU ARE MY ROCK AND MY SAVIOR LORD GOD ALL MIGHTY ABOVE.

ERASING THE HATE I'VE ONCE HAD, REVERSING IT TO LOVE.

I LOVE THE LORD AND ALL THAT HE HAS DONE AND WILL DO.

IF YOU LOVE THE LORD, HE CAN DO THE SAME FOR YOU.

I LOVE THE LORD II

Because of this, I stand by your side.

When things seem tough, I'll just let go of the pride.

Because of this, Anything is possible.

When others use love, they too are able.

When things don't seem to go my way,

I simply get on my knees to pray.

Being thankful that I receive my troubles,

I know that later I'll receive goods in double.

Have love for the Lord & pray.

Don't think about it, start today.

GOD'S FAITHFUL LIL LADY

TAKE MY MIND, MY BODY & MY SOUL.

WHERE EVER YOU LEAD ME, I WILL JOYFULLY GO.

YOU WERE BY MY SIDE THROUGH THICK & THIN.

BECAUSE OF THAT, MY LOVE FOR YOU WILL NEVER EVER END.

THERE'S NO OTHER QUITE LIKE YOURSELF.

YOU'RE THE KING OF KINGS, LORD OF LORDS, NOBODY ELSE.

NO MATTER WHAT, WE STAY ROOTED

LOVE IS NOT ALWAYS HAVING MY WAY, BUT CRUSHING THE HATE AND CONTINUING TO PRAY.

LIFE IS NOT ALWAYS MEANT TO BE PEACHES AND CREAM.

THE TRIALS OF GOD WILL FACE US ALL, BUT OURSELVES WE MUST REDEEM.

WHEN WE DO BAD, GOD DOESN'T LOVE US ANY LESS.

GOD JUST WANTS US TO REPENT AND DO OUR VERY BEST.

SOME PEOPLE BELIEVE YOU GET STRONGER BY WHAT DOES NOT KILL.

I SAY, "JUST MAKE SURE YOU DO GOD'S WILL."

SOME PEOPLE SAY, "NOBODY CAN EVER BE PERFECT LIKE GOD."

I SAY, "JUST TRY, BUT TRY NOT TO BE TOO ODD".

IT'S ALRIGHT, IT'S OKAY BECAUSE A LOT OF FAITH AND PRAYER CAN CHANGE THE DAY.

REMEMBER THAT PATIENCE IS A VIRTUE WHEN PRAYING TO GOD; HOWEVER, GOD WILL DO IF YOU ASK HIM TO AND NOTHING IS TOO HARD.

WHICH WAY SHALL I GO?

THERE'S PAIN AND GUILT BEHIND THESE EYE, BUT ONCE YOU FIND OUT YOU SEEM SURPRISED.

STRUGGLES, HARDSHIPS, CONFUSION WITHIN. WHEN DID IT FIRST OCCUR? WELL, WHERE SHALL I BEGIN?

IT REALLY DOESN'T MATTER NOW. I JUST WANT TO MOVE FORWARD FROM MY MISTAKES.

WHAT I HAVE DISCOVERED IS MAINLY UNDER EXTREME PRESSURE & UNWANTED STRESS, MY SPIRIT BREAKS.

THERE HAVE BEEN MANY HURDLES IN MY LIFE. SOME OBSTACLES EASILY GALLOPED OVER WHILE OTHERS GAVE ME TERRIBLE SCRAPES, CUTTING ME UP LIKE A KNIFE.

OUCH, THAT HURTS AND IT HURTS REALLY BAD. BECAUSE I'M BORDERLINE PERFECTIONIST, I GET CRUSHED AND AM ALL SAD.

IT SEEMS KIND OF FUNNY AS I REVIEW WHAT I WRITE. I CAN SEE CLEARLY NOW WHERE I STAND WITH THE THEORY, "FIGHT OR FLIGHT".

AT THIS POINT IN MY LIFE, I FEEL LIKE THIS IS GETTING OLD. YET THE KEY TO MY LIFE'S PURPOSE, I STILL DO NOT HOLD.

TOO MANY WAYS TO GO, SO I THINK. NOT SURE OF WHICH ROUTE TO TAKE. I JUST DON'T KNOW AS MY LIFE SLOWLY WASHES DOWN THE SINK.

DO I WANT TO WORK IN AN OFFICE, BE A SOLDIER, MODEL OR ACT? RIGHT NOW, I'M WRITING POETRY AND HAVE FOR OVER 15 YEARS. HUMMMMM, A POET. I HAVEN'T THOUGHT OF THAT.

DON'T GET ME WRONG, I AM VERY HAPPY WITH MY LIFE. IT'S JUST THAT I FEEL LIKE A MAP WOULD BE REALLY NICE. SURE THAT'S UNREALISTIC, BUT THAT'S THE LIFE I WANT. INSTEAD OF ACCELERATING, I FEEL AS IF MY SHIP HAS SUNK.

GOD, I NEED MY PURPOSE IN LIFE, SO I CAN FIND MY WAY.

I NEED TO KNOW MY PURPOSE IN LIFE AND I WANT TO KNOW TODAY!

WHO AM I?

WHO AM I?

I AM THE ONE YOU JUST CAN'T FIGURE OUT.

WHO AM I?

I AM THE ONE THAT CAN MAKE THE CROWD SHOUT.

WHO AM I?

I LIVE A SIMPLE LIFE WITH A VISION AND A DREAM.

WHO AM I?

I AM THE ONE BUILDING A HUGE CREATIVE TEAM.

WHO AM I?

I WAS THE ONE HELD BY THE DEVIL, HE LIED.

WHO AM I?

I AM THE EARTH PURIFYING MY VEGETATION

WITH THE SUN GIVING US POWER.

IF YOU'RE NOT GOING TO SUPPLY ME WITH THE

MOTIVATION IN NEED IN LIFE, STEP ASIDE.

I DON'T WANT TO BECOME SOUR.

CHAPTER 2

OVERCOME

BRIGHT LIGHTS, HUNDREDS STARING WITH A CHILL GOING DOWN MY SPINE.

NOT MAKING A SLIP, A FALL OR JUST A MISTAKE IS RACING THROUGH MY MIND.

I MUST IGNORE THE REST & DO MY BEST REMAINING TO BE ONE OF A KIND.

I CAN DO THIS AND I WILL DO THIS RIGHT, ONCE I MAKE UP MY MIND.

STAGE FRIGHT

BRIGHT LIGHTS, HUNDREDS STARTING, AND A CHILL GOING DOWN MY SPINE.

NOT MAKING A SLIP, A FALL OR JUST A MISTAKE IS RACING THROUGH MY MIND.

I'LL IGNORE THE REST AND DO MY BEST.

REMAINING TO BE ONE OF A KIND.

I CAN DO THIS AND I WILL DO THIS RIGHT FROM THE COUNT OF NINE.

WATCH MY WALK, WATCH MY SWAYS, THIS STAGE IS GOING TO BE MINE.

NINE... EIGHT... SEVEN... SIX... FIVE, FOUR, THREE, TWO, ONE.

I PLACE ONE HAND IN MY POCKET WHILE THE OTHER REST ON MY BUN,

THEN ALL OF A SUDDEN, I WALK ADDING A SEXY SLOW RUN.

FEELING GOOD AS THE CROWD BEGAN TO CHEER. OH BOY, I'M HAVING FUN. IF THIS FASHION SHOW WAS A COMPETITION, I DEFINITELY WOULD'VE WON.

ALL I HAD TO DO TO OVERCOME STAGE FRIGHT WAS SIMPLY HAVE FUN.

YOU'RE MAKING YOUR BED

YOUR TIME WILL SURELY COME. REMEMBER THIS DAY WHAT I SAY. HIGH AL-MIGHTY IS YOUR BEING, CASTING DOWN OTHER SUN RAYS.

WICKED LAUGHTER AND SNEAKY WAYS. SOMEONE WILL RISE TO CAST YOU DOWN.

BESIDES, "WHAT GOES AROUND, COMES AROUND".

YOU'RE AS BEAUTIFUL AS A RISING STAR, THE FACE UPON YOUR NECK.

WORDS SPOKEN UPON YOUR LIPS MAKES PEOPLE WANT TO JET.

MUTE TO RESPOND TO YOUR INSULTS AND JUDGMENTAL REMARKS.

FOR YOUR GOAL IS TO HEAD TOWARD THE LIGHT, NOT TOWARD THE DARK.

YOUR TIME WILL SURELY COME. REMEMBER THIS DAY WHAT I SAY.

YOU KNEW THAT ONE DAY YOU WOULD HAVE TO PAY AND GUESS WHAT...

YOU WERE ONCE IN HER SHOES HAVING THE SLIGHTEST IDEA OF WHAT LAY AHEAD.

OH BOY, OH BOY. IF ONLY YOU KNEW, YOU'RE MAKING YOUR BED.

No Pressure

If you can't look me into my eyes,

I can't believe a word you say.

If you can't give me great pleasure,

I may believe you're gay.

If you can't have a conversation with me,

I'll know your patience is lacking within.

If you can't accept my faults in life,

I can't wait to reveal all of you sin.

If you can't stick to what you believe,

I can't be behind you one bit.

If you can't massage my body when I'm feeling drained,

Then baby that's it!

BEEN THERE, DONE THAT. NEXT...

I CAN HONESTLY SAY, I'VE LIVED AN EXCITING LIFE & HAVE SEEN MOST OF THE WORLD.

MEETING MANY WONDERFUL PEOPLE ACROSS THE GLOBE. ACCOMPLISHED MY DREAMS, DATED SOME KINGS & CREATED BEAUTIFUL, TALENTED, STRONG LITTLE QUEENS.

I'M NOT COMPLACENT, I DESIRE AND THIRST FOR MORE; HOWEVER, I AM TRULY SATISFIED WITH WHAT I'M BLESSED TO HAVE. EAGER TO SEE WHAT ELSE IS IN STORE.

I'M AMBITIOUS, FEARLESS, STRONG, COMPETITIVE, ATTRACTIVE & SWEET. THE ONE MAN WHOM DESERVES ME, I HAVE YET TO MEET. IF I CAN BREAK YOU DOWN, SILLY BOY, YOU'RE A CLOWN.

KNEEL DOWN TO THE GROUND, FOR YOU ARE AMONGST A QUEEN. BE STRONG AND SPEAK UP NOW IF YOU BELIEVE YOU DESERVE TO BE CROWNED AS MY KING.

MENTAL QUICK SAND

40 SOMETHING YEAR OLD BOY. WHEN WILL YOU EVER BECOME A MAN? BE LIKE PRESIDENT BARRACK OBAMA & SHOUT, "YES WE CAN". MOVE OUT YOUR FAMILY'S HOUSE, FOR IT'S YOUR MENTAL QUICK SAND.

YOU SPEAK MULTIPLE LANGUAGES & CAN EVEN WRITE IN THOSE LANGUAGES TOO. ONCE YOU PUT YOUR MIND TO IT, THERE'S NOTHING YOU CAN'T DO.

I PRAY THAT ONE DAY YOU'LL DISCOVER YOUR TRUE SELF. MOVE FORWARD IN LIFE, NOT ONLY TO BENEFIT SOMEONE ELSE. YOU'RE SUPPOSED TO BE A KING OR PROVIDER WITH A LADY LIKE ME, BUT WHEN I LOOK INTO YOUR EYES THERE'S A BOY I SEE LOOKING BACK AT ME.

GOD, I PRAY THAT TODAY A CHAIN IS BROKEN. A MAN IS RE-BORN AND IS CAPABLE TO HELP OUT A LADY LIKE ME. DIVORCED WITH THREE CHILDREN TO NOT ONLY FEED, BUT NURTURE, LOVE, MOLD AND LEAD.

THIS TROOP COULD BE YOURS, BUT YOU'RE LACKING WITHIN. LOOKING LIKE A DOG WITH ITS TAIL BETWEEN ITS LEGS WHEN I'M AROUND. LOOKING LIKE ANOTHER 40 SOMETHING YEAR OLD CLOWN.

IT'S NEVER TOO LATE TO MAKE A DIFFERENCE, JUST STOP BEING PHONY. I CAN TELL IF YOU'RE GENUINE OF JUST PLAIN OLE BALONEY.

IT'S TIME TO STAND ON YOUR OWN TWO FEET & BECOME A MAN, PLEASE OF PLEASE BLACK MAN, GET OUT OF YOUR MENTAL QUICK SAND.

CHAPTER 3

EARTH IS NOTHING WITHOUT THE SUN

WHEN I GAZE INTO YOUR EYES, I CAN SEE A BEAST OF ROMANCE, A HAPPY LIFE, AN ON-GOING JOURNEY, PROSPERITY, EXPERIENCES, GROWTH AND LOVE.

WHEN YOU LAY UPON MY LAP, I CAN FEEL CLOSENESS, SENSATION. COMPANIONSHIP AND A DESIRE FOR EXTERNAL PEACE OF MIND, BODY AND SOUL.

WHEN WE HAVE SMALL DISCUSSIONS, I CAN HEAR YOUR MATURITY, INTELLECT, LEADERSHIP, CONFIDENCE, PATIENCE, UNDERSTANDING AND I WILL ABSORB IT ALL.

WHEN OUR SOULS BECOME ONE AND THAT DAY WILL SURELY COME.

ME AS YOUR EARTH AND YOU AS MY SUN, PLANTS WILL GROW IN MORE WAYS THAN ONE.

A HIGH SCHOOL CRUSH

EVERY TIME I SEE YOU,

MY HEART START TO POUND.

I FEEL MYSELF DRIFTING AWAY,

NO LONGER ON THE GROUND.

EVERY TIME YOU LOOK AT ME,

I SMILE WITH SOULFUL DELIGHT.

THIS FEELING DOESN'T GO AWAY,

IT LAST ALL THROUGH THE NIGHT.

THIS HAS NEVER HAPPENED TO ME BEFORE.

I HAVE A SUDDEN FEEL FOR YOU AND DESIRE TO EXPLORE.

I'VE TOLD A COUPLE OF PEOPLE

AROUND ABOUT THIS CRUSH,

BUT THEY WOULD JUST SAY, "THAT IS ONLY LUST". NO!

I HAVE A SUDDEN FEEL FOR YOU

BECAUSE I FEEL THAT YOU ARE TRUE.

IF YOU CANNOT OPEN YOUR MIND,

YOU'LL NEVER SEE THAT I'M 1 OF A KIND.

You Must Be Too Fast

Have you ever met someone who has a rich smile?

The kind that makes you believe that life is actually worthwhile.

Have you ever met someone with a sparkle in their eyes?

Making you want to grab them and unravel them like a package or prize.

Have you ever met someone who can make you go ummmmmmm?

And that's before you two actually make it into the bedroom.

Have you ever met someone and wanted to make it last,

But all of a sudden they become another person of your past?

Stop Giving up that ass.

You must be too fast...

STAY

THIS PLACE IS DARK & A LITTLE SCARY TOO.

I'M SO CONFUSED & DON'T KNOW WHAT TO DO.

I FEEL ALONE OR AT LEAST ONE OF A KIND,

SO CALLED FRIENDS HAVE LEFT ME BEHIND.

WHEN LIFE SEEMED BRIGHTER & IT WAS JUST THE OTHER DAY.

EVERYONE WAS AROUND WITH THEIR CHILDREN READY TO PLAY.

AS SOON AS NEGATIVITY COMES NEARBY TO SAY, "HI".

FRIENDS BEGIN TO DROP LIKE A DEAD FLY.

YOU KNOW WHAT, IT'S ALRIGHT. IT'S OKAY.

BECAUSE PRAYER CAN CHANGE THE DAY.

MY GOD IS BETTER THAN YOU ANYWAY.

LOYAL TO THE END & BETTER THAN A FRIEND.

ALL MY PRAISES GO TO GOD ABOVE.

MY GOD IS NOT DARK, MY GOD IS FULL OF LOVE.

CONFUSION BE GONE, DON'T COME MY WAY.

PEACE, LOVE & HAPPINESS ARE HERE TO STAY.

May "Inner Struggles, Peace & Blessings" open your soul & help you or someone you love to follow your dreams.

That is my intention for anyone reading it.

To experience more, visit:

www.KpPoetry.com

www.instagram.com/Kp.Poetry

https://www.facebook.com/KpPoetry.ISPBbyKp

https://www.youtube.com/channel/UCOubR3C7u4y4HH2I hXlen2g/

#ISPBbyKp

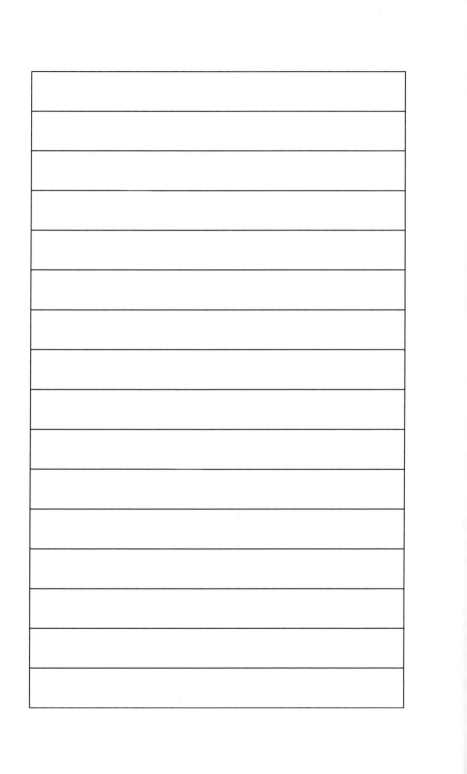